Business and I

FAE (Business Leadership)

Published by
Chartered Accountants Ireland
Chartered Accountants House
47–49 Pearse Street
Dublin 2
www.charteredaccountants.ie

First published 2009
Updated 2012

This publication is designed to provide accurate and authoritative information in regard to the subject matter covered. It is provided on the understanding that the Institute of Chartered Accountants in Ireland is not engaged in rendering professional services. The Institute of Chartered Accountants in Ireland disclaims all liability for any reliance placed on the information contained within this publication and recommends that if professional advice or other expert assistance is required, the services of a competent professional should be sought.

ISBN: 978-1-908199-42-3

Typeset by Deanta Global Publishing Services
Printed by CPI Books Group

Contents

PART III   **FURTHER CASES IN BUSINESS AND ETHICS**

PART I

Introduction

by Gary Martin
Senior Lecturer in Accounting
University of Ulster

updated by Paul Monahan, FCA
Chartered Accountants Ireland

Ethics and the Chartered Accountant

In today's working environment, Chartered Accountants increasingly face pressures that may impact upon their ability to maintain high ethical standards. The challenge for Chartered Accountants is to:

- set high professional, including ethical, standards and live up to them; and
- make the 'right' decision – even if this would personally disadvantage them and/or their firm/employer, i.e. when difficult decisions need to be made (Briers, 2005).

This is why a well-developed ethical awareness on the part of the accountant is of paramount importance.

Ethics, in a professional context, focuses on a code of conduct or a set of moral values that guides our lives and helps us carry out our business (Yaffe, 1996). He further points out that it is defined as principles of honour and morality, accepted rules of conduct, and the moral principles of an individual. Indeed, its centrality to business and the environment in which the accountant plays a key role cannot be underestimated. Guy (1990) remarks that commerce itself depends for its very existence on the ethical behaviour of the participants; for instance, ethical behaviour requires that contracts are honoured, private property is respected, and promises are kept. In this important aspect of commercial and organisational life, the accountant is a key player.

Consequently, the ethical dimension of the work of the professional accountant is significant. As professionals, they serve the public interest. The International Federation of Accountants (IFAC) (2009) defines the public interest as:

> "the collective well-being of the community of people and institutions the professional accountant serves, including clients, lenders, governments, employers, employees, investors, the business and financial community and others who rely on the work of professional accountants."

Cheetham and Chivers (1996) highlight the role of ethics within overall professional competence; specifically, they identify four overlapping sets of values that underpin ethical issues encountered at all levels in the workplace:

- legal values (operating within the law and other mandatory systems);
- professional values (relationships with clients and other professionals);
- organizational values (relationships with colleagues, staff, customers and general public); and
- personal values (individual beliefs and behaviours).

Consequently, Cheetham and Chivers believe ethical judgements make a key contribution to professional performance and ought, therefore, to have an explicit place within any model of professional competence.

In relation to Chartered Accountants specifically, Briers (2005) notes that, in determining whether he or she has made the 'right' decision, the Chartered Accountant should always pause and ask the following important questions:

- Is my decision morally defensible?
- Would a reasonable (and informed) third party reach the same conclusion?
- Will the decision potentially compromise my professional and/or personal reputation? and
- If my decision was subject to public scrutiny would I, my family and my colleagues be proud?

The aim of this text is to:

1. investigate the underpinnings of ethical behaviour;
2. introduce a three-stage ethical decision-making framework to help guide the resolution of potential ethical dilemmas and heighten a sense of practical 'ethical awareness';
3. present a range of fictional, yet potentially real, scenarios, that accountants might face in a variety of settings at various stages of their career; and
4. provide suggestions as to how to approach a general business ethics scenario in an FAE context.

Ethical Behaviour

As Proios (2009) notes, ethics is a philosophical term which derives from the Greek word "ethos" meaning character or custom. Moreover, ethics is a body of principles or standards of human conduct that govern the behavior of individuals and groups. As McPhail and Walters (2009) point out, historically, some of the work in defining ethical issues and working out a response to them was provided by religious institutions and belief systems. Religious systems provided the predominant source of values in the past and, indeed, continue to provide an ethical anchor point for many accountants and business people today (citing Nash, 1994). However, they further draw attention to the fact that many social commentators now suggest that culturally we are living in a post-religious era, citing the work of Alasdair

MacIntyre (1982) when describing the emergence of this new cultural milieu, who connects it with the spread of "moral confusion".

As Thorne, Ferrell and Ferrell (2008) note, many people have justified difficult decisions by citing the golden rule "do unto others as you would have them do unto you" or some other principle. Such principles, or rules, which individuals apply in deciding what is right and wrong, are often referred to as moral philosophies. Most moral philosophies can be classified as:

- consequentialism (encompassing egoism and utilitarianism);
- ethical formalism; or
- justice theory.

Thorne, Ferrell and Ferrell (2008) provide the following definitions:

- **Consequentialism** A class of moral philosophy that considers a decision right or acceptable if it accomplishes a desired result such as pleasure, knowledge, career growth, the realization of self-interest, or utility. Consequentialist theories are also referred to as *teleological ethics*.

    ○ **Egoism** A philosophy that defines right or acceptable conduct in terms of *consequences* for the individual. Egoists believe they should make decisions that maximize their own self-interest, which, depending on the individual, may be defined as physical well-being, power, pleasure, fame, a satisfying career, a good family life, wealth, and so forth.

    ○ **Utilitarianism** This consequentialist philosophy is concerned with seeking the greatest good for the greatest number of people. A utilitarian decision-maker calculates the utility of the consequences of all possible alternatives and then chooses the one that achieves the greatest utility.

- **Ethical Formalism** A class of moral philosophy that focuses on the right of individuals and on the intentions associated with a particular behaviour rather than on its consequences. Ethical formalists regard certain behaviours as inherently right, and their determination of rightness focuses on the individual actor, rather than on society. This moral philosophy stance has been greatly influenced by the work of Immanuel Kant, in particular his "categorical imperative": "Act as if the maxim of your action were to become by your will a universal law of nature." This mode of thinking asks whether the rationale for your action is suitable to become a universal law or principle for everyone to follow. Put another way, this position would lead you to pose the following practical question: "what kind of world would this be if everyone behaved in this way or made this kind of decision in this type of situation?" Ethical formalism is also referred to as *non-consequentialism*, *deontological ethics* and the ethics of respect for persons.

- **Justice Theory** A class of moral philosophy that relates to evaluations of fairness, or the disposition to deal with the perceived injustices of others. Justice, therefore, is more likely to be based on non-consequentialist moral philosophies than on consequentialist philosophies. Different types of justice that can be used to assess fairness in different situations:

- **Distributive justice** evaluates the outcomes or results of a business relationship;
- **Procedural justice** assesses the processes and activities employed to produce the outcomes or results; and
- **Interactional justice** evaluates the communication processes used in the business relationship.

However, it is important to recognize that there is no one 'correct' moral philosophy to apply in resolving ethical and legal issues. It is also important to acknowledge that each philosophy presents an ideal perspective and that most people seem to adapt a number of moral philosophies as they interpret the context of different decision-making situations. Moreover, research suggests that individuals may apply different moral philosophies in different decision situations (Fraedrich and Ferrell, 1992). Each philosophy could result in a different decision in a situation requiring an ethical judgment. And, depending on the situation, people may even change their value structure or moral philosophy when making decisions (Thorne LeClair, Ferrell and Fraedrich, 1998).

McPhail and Walters (2009), for the sake of simplicity, split their consideration of moral philosophy into four broad but distinct perspectives:

1. empirical or descriptive perspectives on how individuals behave in practice;
2. normative perspectives on how individuals should behave;
3. political perspectives – on why in broader social and political terms it's important that individuals behave ethically; and
4. post- and new-modern perspectives – on the prospects of being ethical.

Taking these perspectives forward and translating them into a more applied context, it is useful to review the work of Crane and Matten (2007), who define morality, ethics and ethical theory as follows:

- Morality is concerned with the norms, values and beliefs embedded in social processes which define right and wrong for an individual or a community;
- Ethics is concerned with the study of morality and the application of reason to elucidate specific rules and principles that determine right and wrong for any given situation; and
- These rules and principles are called ethical theories.

This is expressed diagrammatically as follows:

Figure 1: The Relationship between Morality, Ethics and Ethical Theory

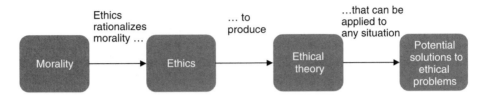

Source: Crane, A. and Matten, D. (2007), *Business Ethics: Managing Corporate Citizenship and Sustainability in the Age of Globalization*, Oxford University Press.

As Crane and Matten further remark, traditional ethical theories – such as those articulated in the definitions by Thorne, Ferrell and Ferrell (2008) above – generally offer a certain rule or principle that can be applied to any given situation. However, they see the limits of traditional theories as being: too abstract; too reductionist; too objective and elitist; too impersonal; too rational and codified. Expressed diagrammatically, traditional ethical theories operate in the following manner:

Figure 2: Traditional Ethical Theories

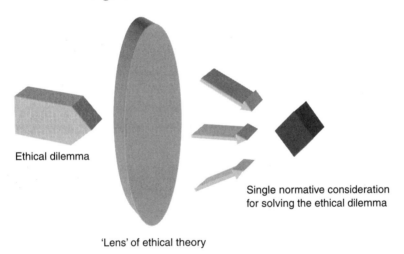

Source: Crane, A. and Matten, D. (2007), *Business Ethics: Managing Corporate Citizenship and Sustainability in the Age of Globalization*, Oxford University Press.

Crane and Matten are advocates of a pluralistic position, arguing that, for the practical purpose of making effective decisions in business, that one theory or one approach will not give the best or true view of a moral dilemma, but suggest, rather that **all** these theoretical approaches will throw light from different angles on one and the same problem and that they should be seen as complementary rather than mutually exclusive. Again, expressed diagrammatically, this position is illustrated as follows:

Figure 3: The Pluralistic Position

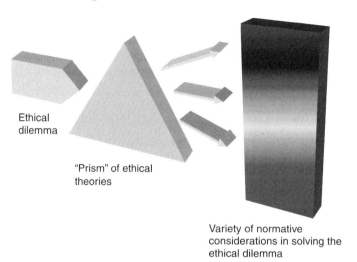

Ethical dilemma

"Prism" of ethical theories

Variety of normative considerations in solving the ethical dilemma

Source: Crane, A. and Matten, D. (2007), *Business Ethics: Managing Corporate Citizenship and Sustainability in the Age of Globalization*, Oxford University Press.

It is important to consider the implications that these types of ethical decision-making have on business and accounting. As Crane and Matten argue, the reasons business ethics is so important can be summarised as follows:

- the power and influence of business in society;
- the potential to make a major contribution to society;
- the potential to inflict harm;
- increasing demands from stakeholders;
- the relative lack of business ethics education or training;
- the continued occurrence of ethical infractions;
- in evaluating different ways of managing business ethics; and
- because it is interesting and rewarding.

As McPhail and Walters (2009) remark, while this increased technical complexity has focused attention on the competence of accountants and the profession's requisite body of knowledge, these issues also problematize the profession's public interest claims. For example, while resolving the issue of how companies account for pensions requires a fairly advanced level of technical competence, the emotive and very civic nature of the issue also problematizes the profession's claim to be acting in the public interest. McPhail and Walters further argue that, despite the general increase in ethical awareness, the growing pervasiveness and complexity of multinational business and the rising importance of accounting all come at a time when many moral philosophers are suggesting that our traditional ethical resources have been undermined. Yet, they are not suggesting that accountants as individuals lack the capacity to recognize what is good behaviour and act on it. As they point out:

> "… rather, our concern lies with the ability to analyse accounting ethically within its broader organizational and political/economic context … to get you thinking about the broader ethical issues related to the function of accounting and our claim to be professionals who have the public interest at heart."

The ethical dilemmas case studies that follow in Parts II and III will present some practical characteristics of these attributes, with a view to refining and enhancing levels of ethical awareness. As Guy (1990) notes, making ethical decisions is easier said than done, pointing out that few people intentionally set out to be unethical. Yet, as she further remarks, often day-to-day activities lead people to succumb to expedient decisions which have less than ethical consequences, concluding that "competent, successful managers must plant their feet firmly in the practical world of compromise and expediency". The successful and competent accountant, no matter where they operate, must also function in the same, potentially dangerous, terrain. To make this journey less fraught, the following decision-making framework seeks to act as a guide for the ethical dilemmas that then follow.

An Ethical Decision-making Framework: A Three-step Approach

In developing a practical, ethical decision-making framework, it is useful to consult the three approaches below in conjunction with one another:

- the first is the fundamental principles of the Chartered Accountants Ireland *Code of Ethics* (2011);
- the second is Hodgson's three-stage framework (1992); and
- the third is Blanchard and Peale's ethics check (1998).

Step 1
Fundamental Principles (Code of Ethics, Effective July 2011)

(a) Integrity

A professional accountant should be straightforward and honest in all professional and business relationships.

(b) Objectivity

A professional accountant should not allow bias, conflict of interest or undue influence of others to override professional or business judgements.

(c) Professional Competence and Due Care

A professional accountant has a continuing duty to maintain professional knowledge and skill at the level required to ensure that a client or employer receives competent professional service based on current developments in practice, legislation and techniques. A professional accountant should act diligently and in accordance with applicable technical and professional standards when providing professional services.

(d) Confidentiality

A professional accountant should respect the confidentiality of information acquired as a result of professional and business relationships and should not disclose any such information to third parties without proper and specific authority unless there is a legal or professional right or duty to disclose. Confidential information acquired as a result of professional and business relationships should not be used for the personal advantage of the professional accountant or third parties.

(e) Professional Behaviour

A professional accountant should comply with relevant laws and regulations and should avoid any action that discredits the profession.

Step 2
Hodgson's Three-Stage Framework (1992)

1. Examine the situation:
   - Get the critical facts.
   - Identify the key stakeholders.
   - Identify each stakeholder's options (what each stakeholder wants done).
2. Establish the dilemma:
   - Identify the working principles and norms that drive each option (why each stakeholder wants it done).
   - Project the possible outcomes (consequences) of each stakeholder option. Do any violate your principles, or those of your organisation?
   - Determine the actions (means) necessary to produce each outcome. Do any violate your principles, or those of your organisation?
   - State the dilemma.
3. Establish the options:
   - Identify the general principles(s) behind each option.
   - Compare the general principle(s) behind each option. Which is the most responsible general principle(s) in this situation?

The option with the most responsible general principle(s) is your choice for action.

But before you make your final decision, follow …

Step 3
Blanchard and Peale's Ethics Check (1998)

1. Is it legal? Will I be violating either civil law or company policy?

2. Is it balanced? Is it fair to all concerned in the short term as well as the long term? Does it promote win-win relationships?

3. How will it make me feel about myself? Will it make me feel proud? Would I feel good if my decision were published in the newspaper? Would I feel good if my family knew about it?

How to Lay Out a Solution to a General Business Ethics Indicator in an FAE Exam

In planning the layout of your solution to a general business ethics indicator in an FAE exam context, it is important to recognise that solutions to general business ethics issues are different to many other issues in the FAE. Typically, they will be different even from indicators on professional ethics or corporate governance. Indicators on general business ethics are different because there are no 'rules' as such, and often no absolute 'right' or 'wrong' answers. In these circumstances, the 'process' becomes more important and it is essential that you demonstrate your thought process to the examiner in a structured and logical manner. What is not required is a general, unstructured essay with a conclusion (arbitrary or otherwise) tacked on to the end.

The approach suggested here (and this is just one, there are others) is to plan and structure your answer so that the examiner can see the following five elements of the process:

1. **Identify the critical facts** Demonstrate that you have recognised the key issues in the dilemma you are facing.

2. **Identify the stakeholders** It is important to recognise all parties affected by your decision, which may include society as a whole. Remember, as aspiring professional Chartered Accountants you have a duty to the public as well as to your clients and your employer.

3. **What are the options available to the decision-maker?** Show that you have considered all options, not just the choice you finally settle on.

4. **Set out the arguments for and against** Effectively what are the key influences on your decision – the 'three-step approach' on Page 7 above will be very helpful here – the dilemma you are posed is likely to have 'shades of grey' rather than be clearly 'black' or 'white'. Alternatively, use a recognised ethical decision making model to assist you building your reasoning and reaching a conclusion.

5. **Provide your decision, conclusion or recommendation** Do not try to hide from the need to conclude.

Ethical Dilemmas

Part II contains a series of ethical dilemmas. At the end of each dilemma, the case states that the next step in the decision-making process is "over to you". You should use the decision-making framework outlined in Part I, as well as your own experience, to guide your deliberations.

(Suggested solutions to these dilemmas are available from your lecturer.)

1. An Inspector Calls

Kevin is a Chartered Accountant who qualified 18 months ago. Though he had qualified as an accountant in a small practice in Dublin, it was always his intention to work as an accountant in business. Given the downturn in the economy in recent times, he had decided to bide his time. After all, his firm renewed his contract on a two-year temporary basis. So he decided to stay where he was, waiting for a suitable opportunity to come along in the business field, maybe manufacturing, when things picked up.

A few months ago now, much to his surprise, he noticed a job for an assistant accountant with a manufacturing company. The ad grabbed his attention for a number of reasons. First, it was an opportunity to join an up-and-coming manufacturing company, and to get into an area of work that he really was interested in. Secondly, it was closer to where he was living; he would save half an hour commute each way, every day. And, third, there was the pay: it was considerably more than he was currently earning. Though this initially struck him as a bit odd in the current downturn, he thought he would apply. He was invited to interview and, after going to an initial, and then a follow-up interview, he was offered a job with the company.

He was very pleased at this unexpected opportunity, though he did continue to have some reservations. Though he thought that the office seemed somewhat "chaotic" on the occasions he visited, he convinced himself that there would be some plausible explanation for this: it was probably just month-end related activity and it wouldn't be as stressful as that when he started. After all, he was a qualified accountant and had dealt with a few difficult situations in the course of his work in the practice. How hard could it be?

After six weeks in the job, alarm bells began to ring for Kevin about how the business was being run. First, there was the lack of qualified accountants. Apart from the finance director, he appeared to be the only one in what was a busy accounts office. Furthermore, it had become clearer since he started that he had been brought in to "firefight" on a number of fronts. It appeared that relationships with a number of government and statutory agencies had become strained; completion dates for a variety of returns and submissions had fallen behind and, as a result, the company needed the "kudos" of a qualified accountant to sort the problems out.

So, it became clear that Kevin was expected to play a leading role in "sorting the place out". Though this aspect of the job wasn't highlighted at the interview, Kevin had to get used to working through the issues as best he could, one by one. Though he had uncovered no evidence of wrong-doing, just general chaos, he nonetheless regretted giving up his more secure, less well paid job for this. However, as his friend Shane told him: "you've made your bed, now you have to lie in it".

Kevin persuaded himself that a few late nights, combined with a few weekends' work, would set everything straight. Once this was done, he could settle down and start to enjoy what he had thought the job entailed. Until he got to that point, he just had to keep his head down and get on with it. Despite the work-related pressure, he enjoyed the general atmosphere in the firm. It would be worth it in the end, he kept telling himself.

On one of the evenings he was working on the backlog, he went out to grab a bite to eat at about 6pm. He got back for 7 and intended to stay on for just another hour or so. Rome wasn't built in a day, after all, and he would be in on Saturday in any case. He would work his way through things bit by bit. He was just about to head home for the evening when the phone rang. It was security. Visitors had arrived in reception looking to speak to someone in accounts. It was important they speak to someone, they said. Wishing he had let the call go, Kevin nonetheless said he would go down to speak to the mystery visitors, despite the odd time of night for accounts to be receiving guests. He was shocked when he heard that they were from the Fraud Squad and had a warrant to search the premises in connection with alleged irregularities within the firm. Kevin, who had never noticed or seen anything in the company that really worried him, and who was looking forward to getting home to relax at the end of another stressful day, now had a serious dilemma about what he ought to do.

Over to you …

2. Keeping it in the Family

Kerry is a Chartered Accountant, employed as an audit manager. She was one of the first members of her family to go to college and, after university, she embarked on a training contract with a large accountancy practice. She enjoyed the challenge of professional study, even though the schedule of work and exams could be gruelling at times.

Though she worked for a large practice that had a national presence, she had requested a transfer to work in one of their regional offices. The regional office had a client base that was made up principally of small- and medium-sized enterprises, a mixture of retail and manufacturing businesses; indeed, many of the companies were well known to her, as she had grown up in the town next to where the office was located. Despite the fact that she had lived, and enjoyed, the "big city" experience when at university, she was happy moving back to work near the town where she had grown up. The familiarity of small town life, and having her family nearby, was something she really appreciated and this helped her settle into her training and professional life.

Indeed, the occasion of Kerry's qualification as a Chartered Accountant had been a cause of much celebration for her immediate family, extended family and friends. They had even thrown her a party at the time. Since then, if any of her family members had any financial queries, they would run them by her: she was the "financial expert" after all. To date, although they had all been straightforward queries, she was uncomfortable at times at being seen as the "financial oracle". However, she felt obliged to help. They had been helpful to her when she was studying and training. What's more, she was back now living among her family and community and wanted to do her best to build her reputation in the local area.

Fortunately, she had never been asked directly for investment advice. This would have created a problem for her as she felt that, being an auditor, rather than a registered financial adviser, this would be beyond her competence. Then, however, her aunt Eleanor asked to see her one weekend about a financial matter that she would prefer "to keep between ourselves". Though close to her aunt, Kerry felt nonplussed at the request. She had never discussed financial matters with Eleanor before. She hoped that it would be something straightforward.

Kerry's concerns, however, proved to be well-founded. Eleanor told Kerry that she had come into a significant amount of money on the winding-up of Seamus's estate. She hadn't rushed into making rash decisions about what to do with the money, but she felt that she now wanted to invest. Moreover, she proceeded to tell her niece that she wanted to put the money into a general store in a neighbouring town. Eleanor had been a loyal customer of the shop for the past 25 years or so and, as a result, had got to know the owners well. They were a couple she met socially in the town from time to time, and were people she felt she could trust. She told Kerry that she wanted to invest 80% of her funds and felt this could be the ideal opportunity. The business was well-established with an apparently loyal customer base; the people who ran the business were individuals of good standing that she felt she could trust; and, given the location of the business, she would be close at hand to monitor its progress.

Kerry has concerns on two levels: first, being asked to give advice on such an extensive and substantial investment; and secondly, she was the audit manager who worked on the audit of the general store. From her knowledge of the firm's trading activities, she knew the commercial realities facing the firm. She didn't think that the owners were trying to mislead her aunt; like Eleanor, she knew them to be people who were well-respected in the local community. She did, however, know that sales had been declining for the last number of years, and that the business was suffering from significant cash flow problems. Commercially, while many of their customers liked the unchanging pace and character of the shop, this didn't necessarily translate into sales; customers tended to use it for small purchases, rather than their weekly shop. Kerry also knew that this situation would get significantly worse if planning permission for the supermarket on the outskirts of town was granted by the Council. Eleanor, unaware that Kerry has any particular insight into the specifics of this business, has asked her what she thinks she should do. Kerry now has a dilemma.

Over to you …

3. Buy to Let or Buy to Loot?

Paula is a Chartered Accountant who, since qualification, has specialized in tax and worked for a medium-sized practice. Most of her clients comprise a mixture of micro and small enterprises and individuals who need advice on their tax affairs. Her sister, Linda, has asked her to do her tax return. Paula has done the tax return in the past without any issue or problem. Though Paula had initially asked herself if it would be appropriate to provide professional services to a family member, she didn't see any great problem, given the straightforward nature of the work involved. Also, given the fact it was her sister, she was well aware of her personal circumstances and knew that she wasn't hiding anything from her, even though Linda could be a bit disorganised at times.

Linda is self-employed and has never had problems in relation to money in the past; she has always been fairly comfortably off. In the midst of the property boom of the early 2000s, she bought two houses as investments. Though everyone seemed to be building up a property portfolio at the time, Linda had a more pressing issue for wishing to invest in property. Being self-employed, she should have been making provision for her pension more conscientiously, but she hadn't. As a result, she had a pension shortfall. This led directly to her decision to put her money into bricks and mortar. She bought one property in a new development, let it and, with the proceeds she built up, decided to put a deposit down on a second property.

As the good times continued, money was plentiful for Linda, financing a lifestyle that included regular European city breaks, in addition to a three-week summer holiday. Fixtures and fittings in her rental properties were of the highest standard, and no expense was spared. Paula kept telling her sister that she should be putting aside a bit of rainy day money. But Linda wasn't really listening; she was making so much as an amateur property developer that her thoughts were more in the "here and now", rather than the medium or longer term. The Celtic Tiger was roaring and trying to hear above the din was difficult. As Linda would often say to Paula, "the good times are here to stay!"

Then, even as property prices started to cool in 2007–08, Linda thought she would take on a further house, before some of the "buy to let" deals disappeared. Now she had a property portfolio of three houses, but was saddled with high levels of debt. She was so highly leveraged, and her mortgage repayments so finely balanced, that any change at all in circumstances could lead to difficulties. But, as she said at the time, so far, so good. Initially, Linda did not appear to be greatly affected by the downturn.

As we all know the property market collapsed, almost completely and rapidly, and tenants that Linda had in the good times started to disappear. Compounding this problem was the fact that Linda lived in a rural location that did not have a plentiful supply of replacement tenants. Things were getting grim. The mainstay of her business in the past had been the steady flow of workers employed in the construction of new properties. But now, in severe downturn, and in a double blow to Linda, some of those working and renting left, leaving few options for recruiting new tenants.

Linda has been experiencing financial difficulties in recent months. To make ends meet, she has been using the entire rental income from her properties to service their mortgages. And obviously, despite the straitened financial circumstance she finds herself in, she still must pay tax on the rental income.

However, a consequence of the worsening housing market is that Linda hasn't been setting money aside to pay her tax liabilities from her rental income. When she leaves the papers around for her sister to prepare the tax return, Paula notices that all details for her third, newest property are missing. Noticing this omission, she phones her sister and asks for the relevant paperwork. Linda says she will meet Paula for a coffee and give her the necessary documentation then. Paula thinks nothing more of it assuming Linda must have forgotten to include the necessary papers.

As arranged, Paula meets Linda for coffee on Saturday morning and asks for the papers. Linda tells Paula about her difficulties and that this matter has been playing on her mind for some time. She then asks Paula if she could prepare the return using the information she has at hand, without details of the third property. "Pretend you don't know about it. Sure, how would they ever know about it? Take a chance, they'll never find out."

Paula is very concerned about her sister's request. Whilst she knows she can be a bit disorganised, she never envisioned this, effectively being party to tax evasion. Added to the conflict Paula faces, she is also mindful of the possible employment consequences if anything went wrong. Paula's employer doesn't know she has been effectively "moonlighting". To make matters worse, she read an article recently describing how that the tax authorities are in the process of clamping down on "amateur property developers" as they suspect a lot of tax is being evaded in this area of economic activity. Paula is in a dilemma.

Over to you …

4.   **Not a Petty Matter**

Siobhan, a trainee accountant, has a hunch about something that has been happening in the office. For a few weeks now, there has been a problem that is poisoning the atmosphere there. Alleged thefts have been reported from the petty cash box. The manager gathered the staff together for a meeting a week ago and told everyone that, much to his surprise and disappointment, thefts had apparently been occurring.

Siobhan suspects that it may be Emmet, a fellow trainee. Recently, on a social night out after work, she noticed that Emmet appeared a bit "flush". She wondered how this could be. After all, they were on the same rate of pay, and she had difficulty meeting her bills every month. What's more, yesterday lunchtime, she met him on the street coming out of the bookies.

Since starting on the same day, last September, Siobhan and Emmet have never really got on. She thinks he is a bit of a "wide boy", "in love with the sound of his own voice". He's not her type of person. This fact notwithstanding, the petty cash problem is starting to get on her nerves. It's the talk of the place. She wishes it would just go away. But the manager has effectively set a deadline of 10 days for the person involved to make themselves known to him. She now has to weigh up whether she reports her suspicion or says nothing?

What evidence can she point to? Is there a reasonable suspicion, and is this sufficient to report a serious allegation? As Siobhan is well aware, impugning a colleague's reputation is a very serious issue. She vaguely remembers that the company has a whistleblowing policy – she remembers glancing at it when she started. She thinks that, from what she read, it made some reference to the company taking very seriously any allegation of misconduct, but also the consequences of malicious allegations. If she is wrong, she could end up being disciplined. What's not very helpful in the whistleblowing policy is the lack of clear examples to guide someone in making a well-balanced decision.

Siobhan now is in a real dilemma: how might the issue be viewed, or dealt with, under the terms of the whistleblowing policy? Would this be an acceptable way to proceed? She is concerned about balancing the rights of the individual employee, who is a rival, and, for that matter, someone she doesn't particularly like, and the problem that the company is investigating which, after all, is potentially a crime. Then again, can Siobhan be sure that thefts have taken place? Might there be a plausible alternative explanation, a systems problem, for instance, that gives the impression of a shortfall, yet might mask other problems? What if she makes these allegations and this turns out to be the case. Siobhan is in a dilemma.

Over to you …

5. Time After Time

Ryan is an audit manager, recently recruited to the firm. He has moved from another part of the country and has taken this job after being made redundant by his previous firm. He was disappointed by being let go by his previous firm and had been out of work for about nine months before getting this new job. It became more and more dispiriting dealing with rejection letter after rejection letter. After eight months of soul-destroying searching, he was delighted to get this opening: it was good to be working again. Given the perilous state of the economy, he was going to do everything to keep this job. Since starting, he has fitted in well. He really wants to give a good impression and is eager to learn "how things are done" in the firm. He wants he wants to be "one of us".

Towards the end of a long and complex engagement, he is managing a job that has run over budget. Given the general downturn in the economy, he didn't want to flag to the client that the job would go over budget. He did mention it to the assistant audit director responsible for the audit who told him not to worry; it "would be fixed". He didn't query what this meant; he assumed that he would get a bit of wriggle room to work with in his hours. He thought that a way would be found to flex his budget to allow for the overrun to be accommodated.

At the end of the job, he found out that things weren't going to be so easy to sort out. He was told to charge the overrun to a variety of other clients. The work had been done but the clients on the current job have queried bills in the past. Indeed, they could get quite aggressive in relation to billing and revelled in going through the bill, line by line, to query items. They were, nonetheless, a big client for the firm and, in the current economic climate, they didn't want to lose such a valuable client. The assistant audit director tells Ryan to spread the cost across a number of clients, but to be sure not to make it too obvious.

The job finished recently, and the bill is to be submitted to the potentially difficult clients. Ryan felt quite uneasy at this type of practice. He has never countenanced doing this before, and has never been asked to do this at other firms he worked for. To make the situation worse, Ryan now faces some additional pressures. Since his discussion with the assistant audit director, he has found out that: (i)the client now wants a discount on his fee, owing to financial pressures; and (ii) his assistant audit director is going for promotion as an audit director. Ryan is in a dilemma.

Over to you …

6.   Beyond Budgeting

Sonya is a Chartered Accountant who moved into industry after qualifying 10 years ago. She was typical of a Chartered Accountant who wanted to get the thorough grounding and insight into business training in practice gave her, and then move into mainstream commercial activity, rather than stay in practice.

Initially, she joined an insurance company with a national presence. Since this initial post, she has had a variety of jobs that have steadily built her commercial skills. She has ambitions to move up the career ladder. She hopes someday to become a main board director. Aware that this would be her ultimate aim, she needed to broaden her skills set and her commercial competencies. Her latest promotion saw her become a regional sales director, leading a sales force of 30 sales staff in her area. She enjoys the challenge this commercial role provides, as well as the opportunity to develop her profile within the company.

Later this year, the commercial director on the board, her line manager, is due to retire. She is seen as being in the running for the soon-to-become-vacant position of commercial director. She was quietly confident that she would be able to put forward a good application when the time came. However, in the meantime, the commercial director is keen to review current year income against budget, as part of the budget process for the following year for his division. The commercial director calls Sonya in and tells her he wants to make sure she helps him to protect the division's budget for next year. He has told her that the finance director is on the warpath and is determined to slash annual budgets across the board.

The commercial director, mindful of what any diminution of his budget would do to his standing in the company pecking order, puts Sonya under pressure to accrue expenses – he doesn't want to lose any of their budgets. He also wants to protect his "turf"; he reminds Sonya where her loyalties should lie.

Sonya is told that her efforts for the "greater good of the division", as he puts it, will not go unnoticed. In her professional opinion as an accountant, she is not convinced at all that the expenses will crystallize.

She is a member of Chartered Accountants Ireland and, just because she works in a commercial rather than a financial role, this does not mean she can ignore her professional obligations. Though she has been assiduously building up her profile as a loyal and committed company servant, she knows that she is still bound by the values and principles of being a Chartered Accountant. What should she do next? She is expected to have a good chance in the forth-coming promotion round, and is relying on a recommendation from her manager. She feels torn. Sonya is in a dilemma.

Over to you …

7.   When Harry, the Manager, Met Sally, the Trainee...

As part of the process of "socialising" new recruits to a large company, the directors had arranged a "get to know you" session. It was held at a local hotel and was a very convivial event: wine, canapés, and so forth. The evening finished at about 8.30pm with a motivational speech from the human resources director, who told the assembled audience of trainees, directors and managers that he was very happy with the recruitment process during the last year, that the company was delighted to recruit people of such high quality, and that a warm welcome would await them. He half-jokingly referred to the fact that some of the new recruits would get to know other members of staff better than their own friends and their nearest and dearest, given the hours they would be working together. The audience gave a nervous laugh, half hoping he wasn't really serious. For one trainee, Sally, 24, this observation was prescient.

Sally followed some of her new colleagues to a nearby bar for a drink after all the "stuffy suits" went home. This was an exciting time, especially after what she saw as the drudgery of university life. It wasn't the experience itself she found dispiriting; it was the experience of "being broke" that really got to her. Yes, working as a trainee accountant wasn't exactly what she needed to solve all her financial foibles, but it would do nicely for the next few years, even though she wasn't looking forward to the exams.

While at the party, she met Harry, one of the managers, who had also attended the hotel function. Harry is 35, has been with the company since joining as a trainee himself, and is generally seen as a "safe pair of hands". He is popular with his peers and is a member of staff whom everyone gets on with. He is popular with the firm's hierarchy too, and seen as something of a rising star. He and Sally got chatting in the bar that evening, and seemed to have a lot in common, despite the age gap. It turns out that they attended the same school and a lot of the conversation that night focused on mutual acquaintances and which teachers they had during their respective times at the school. It was a good evening, and they got on very well. Just as the evening was about to end, Harry mentioned to Sally that they should meet up some time for a coffee. Having had a genuinely enjoyable evening, she looked forward to bumping into Harry again. She thought he was a nice guy, and that knowing him would help her fit in to the new office. Everything was falling into place.

Harry, though a manager in the firm, was not Sally's line manager. Neither he, nor she, felt it inappropriate to have coffee now and again. The only thing that concerned them was if people thought she was being treated favourably, but nobody really passed any comment on the matter. After all, when they had coffee, Sally's best friend, Carol, another trainee, was nearly always there, so no eyebrows were ever raised.

However, Carol, upon borrowing Sally's company laptop one day to visit a client, got a bit of a surprise, one that Sally hadn't confided in her. Upon powering up the laptop, connections to a messaging service used by Sally appeared automatically, along with messages she had been sharing with Harry. Though she did not intentionally go looking for the files, she read what appeared on the screen. It was apparent that Harry and Sally had been dating, due to the intimate nature of the messages they had been exchanging. She couldn't believe that Sally hadn't told her what was happening. Over the past few weeks, she effectively went "off radar" at lunchtime; she was never free to go to the gym at lunchtime any more – she must have been meeting up with Harry. It was clear too, from the messages on the laptop, that, as well as having an intimate relationship with Sally, Harry was worried what other people would think, and wanted to keep the arrangement secret. They weren't going to tell anyone about their relationship.

Carol is now in a dilemma. Should she confront Sally about what is going on? Should she tell anyone else about what has been happening? She is intrigued as to why Harry wants to keep things secret – what have they to hide? She once heard it said that, in becoming a good professional, transparency was a fundamental principle in conducting yourself in work situations. But she is confused by the turn of events – was it any of her business, was it any of the companys's business, or should she just leave well enough alone? Carol is in a dilemma.

Over to you ...

8. Called to Account

Maria is a senior in a large accounting practice. She works in a small, relatively happy team that, prior to the last few weeks, had been getting on well with one another. Another senior in the team, Alan, has asked Maria if he could have a meeting with her to discuss a confidential and sensitive issue. Though Alan is a rival to Maria in relation to the forthcoming round of promotions, she wouldn't say that she didn't get on with him, just that she was pretty indifferent towards him; you don't necessarily have to like the people you work with, after all. That is why the request for the meeting was all the more surprising. 'What does he want?' she thought to herself.

She agreed to meet him when she was next in the office. Alan spoke to her in hushed tones. Whatever it was, it had had a profound effect on him. He calmly, yet resolutely, told Maria that he was going to go to Erin, their partner, and their manager Brian's boss, to make an informal complaint of bullying by Brian. He told Maria how Brian's behaviour in recent weeks was becoming more and more intolerable, to the extent that Alan had a knot in his stomach coming into work every day. While she sympathised with Alan and the circumstances he described, she couldn't help wondering inwardly: "where exactly is he going with this, and why does he want to involve me?" She didn't have to wait too long for these questions to be answered.

Alan then quickly told Maria that he believed she could help him. He had kept a record of the allegations he was going to put in his complaint. He had noted days, times, topics, every conceivable detail. Alan told her that though she obviously wasn't present on each and every occasion he felt he had been bullied by Brian, he believed her corroborating evidence to strengthen his story would be beneficial, and would she be prepared to provide this? Maria didn't know quite what to say. She couldn't recall any explicit events where she thought Brian had overstepped the mark with Alan in relation to his behaviour. Alan had obviously perceived things quite differently.

While she saw Brian's blunt brusqueness as perhaps jolting at times, Alan obviously thought his behaviour was nit-picking and deliberately undermining him in carrying out his role. Maria told Alan she would think overnight on what he had said and get back to him tomorrow. When she got home, Maria was no clearer about how to proceed. Whatever came to pass, she would obviously state the facts as she saw them, clearly and unambiguously. But how are you meant to deal with a situation where differing perceptions were in play? And how would she be affected by the fallout of the complaint? She had read something in a Sunday supplement recently about how fractious and unpleasant grievances in the workplace could be. Furthermore, she wasn't even sure Brian was guilty of bullying Alan – besmirching someone's reputation is a serious issue, did Alan fully understand the implications of his planned action? What's more, Brian was due to write up Maria's final probationary report in two weeks, which would confirm her permanent appointment. Maria is in a dilemma.

Over to you …

9. Party Games

Sue, an audit manager with a medium-sized accountancy practice, has been working as the audit firm's main liaison at the audit of a designer shoe chain for the last two years. From what

Sue has seen, the client runs an impressive operation. The client is well respected, ethical and likes to have everything "just right". The client makes a great play about sourcing clothes from ethical supply chains; as a result, the firm has built up a brand that is thriving given the affluent demographics they service despite the recession.

The audit is also a favourite of the entire audit team given the happy work environment apparent in the firm. Sue's team genuinely gets on well with the management in the client office and, overall, it is one of her favourite jobs. The past financial year has been successful for the firm. As a "thank you" for a job well done, the client has invited Sue and the team to their annual party (for management and staff). The audit process itself has gone well; all of the work has been completed on time and within budget. Sue is aware of the importance of this client to the audit firm and is in something of a quandary. She is concerned about her ethical responsibility but her partner reminds her that it is important to network and maintain good client relations.

The audit team is looking forward to going to the party. Given the clientele the firm services, there are rumours that some celebrities will be at the party. The chief executive sees nothing wrong with inviting the auditors; she sees them as key stakeholders of the firm, a stakeholder group she should engage with actively. Indeed, she sees the event as nothing more than another networking event that she holds frequently.

Sue is still in two minds about what to do. On the morning of the day before the party, Andrea, the chief executive, calls her to confirm the numbers coming. When Sue sees that it is Andrea calling, she asks one of her colleagues to answer the call and take a message. She is pondering what to do. However, Andrea has just made another offer that complicates matters further. She leaves a message that the audit party should come early and have a look around the store before the party starts – she is leaving instructions that they can select some products and they will get a discount at the till. Sue now is in a real dilemma. Given her concerns about how this all might look, especially to those at the audit firm, and outside the firm, what should she now do? Sue is in a dilemma.

Over to you …

10. Poetic Licence

Kirsty is a new trainee in the audit department. She started with the firm six months ago and, slowly but surely, is coming to grips with the challenging nature of new work schedules and working on a wide variety of jobs. She finds it very different from university and, though she feels it will take a while to get really settled in, she's glad that she gets on so well with everyone in the team she is working with, especially Rory, her senior. Rory has been very easy to work with and to deal with and she has looked up to him since starting. He is knowledgeable, well-prepared and takes time to help out whenever Kirsty has a query. In effect, he has been the ideal mentor. Though she got two job offers before joining the firm, she is pleased to be here, and is convinced she had made the right choice.

As well as all of the technical skills she is acquirng, she is also developing her interpersonal skills. In preparing for her job interviews, she had read a lot about the need for accountants to develop "softer" skills, as well as the "hard" technical knowledge that was expected of them. Though she had got on with people reasonably well throughout her school and university years, she was a bit daunted at how this might pan out in a work setting. She felt she had no need to worry; she didn't foresee having to deal with any difficult conflict situation, as she loved working in and with the team. And if anything looked like it was potentially going to go wrong, she could turn to Rory for advice. Having that welcoming environment and back-up made going to work every day that bit more pleasant. In essence, as well as liking the people she worked with, she essentially trusted them and their judgement.

Two days ago, this aspect of Kirsty's personality – wanting to see the best in people – was given a severe jolt. She was checking her voicemail and, much to her surprise, there was a message from Patrick, her team's manager. The message was abrupt, and Kirsty could feel the tension in Patrick's voice: "Would you give me a ring to make an appointment to see me, there is something I need to discuss with you". What was this all about? Kirsty had absolutely no idea. What would a manager want to discuss directly with a trainee, surely they should go through the senior first? She found it remarkable that she should be on Patrick's radar, never mind his requesting a meeting with her, and it wasn't remarkable in a good way. In a bit of a panic, she phoned Rory, nervously asking what could this all mean? Rory calmed the waters and was, in Kirsty's words, a "rock of sense". He told her it was probably a "get to know you" chat as Patrick hadn't had an opportunity to get to know the new trainees properly at the induction session. She made the appointment, noted the time in her diary and thought nothing more of it.

Fast forward two days. Kirsty is sitting across from Patrick's cavernous desk and is being berated for her minimal contribution to the team. He shows her the files for the big job the team has just finished. To her horror, Rory has changed her initials on the working papers. It is starting to dawn on her that he must have been slacking on the job, and now wanted to pass her work off as his. What's more, Patrick tells Kirsty that he has already discussed this matter with Rory, and Rory was at a loss to know what Kirsty had been doing too. Patrick has told her that, by the end of the day, he wants a full account of everything she had done to justify the hours, especially as the job went over budget. Kirsty is distraught; she was working hard with people she liked, building up working relationships based on trust. This trust has now been cruelly betrayed, landing Kirsty in trouble. What should she do now? Kirsty is in a dilemma.

Over to you …

11. "Just Sign on the Dotted Line …"

Sean started five months ago with a small practice. His manager, Pauline, is great to get on with. She is very much in favour of an informal culture in the office. Sean has responded well to this trust and integrity his manager has placed in him and the rest of the team. But Sean is getting a bit concerned about what he sees as the downside of this informality. Another student, Michelle, has told him that Pauline isn't that bothered about the CA Diary – "she'll sign off on it regardless of what you put in it". It seems Pauline wants to be everyone's friend, and one of the ways it would appear she was trying to do this is to sign off the diaries with little or no scrutiny. As Michelle told Sean "Sure it's only a box-ticking exercise anyway, what does it matter? There's no harm being done and you'll never get caught".

This is now at the point where a number of the students are capitalising on the situation and recording inflated accounts of experience – particularly in auditing. This is particularly serious, as this experience counts towards the auditing certificate. Sean is coming under pressure to "join in", but to him it appears that trust is being breached. He is aware of the implications of being found out, both in terms of a disciplinary offence, and the lasting impact on his reputation. He also sees Pauline's practices as a false economy. This type of approach will only lead to gaps in their technical knowledge and competence. The only people who will benefit are lazy members of staff, who are not fit for purpose. He also remembers an old adage, "those you can trust with small things are those you can trust with the big things". But, although he wants to do something about the situation, the team and Pauline socialise on a Friday after work and he fears being ostracised. Sean is in a dilemma.

Over to you …

12. Speaking Truth to Power

Laurence is a senior in a medium-sized accountancy practice. Andrew, one of the juniors, has come to him with an issue that is troubling him. Andrew has seen a manager re-performing on a file some financial reporting work he had completed. Andrew doesn't understand why their treatment of the work has been amended. He tells Laurence that the manager simply took the file, reviewed the contents and told him he was making some changes. He made no effort to discuss this with Andrew; he just inexplicably made the changes.

When Laurence looked through the work, he realised that the manager had reached an incorrect conclusion and that Andrew the junior's work was actually correct. The particular manager was recently promoted and is senior to Laurence in the firm. Laurence has heard rumblings about this particular manager before; office gossip has it that he is a "bit flaky", and "promoted above his pay grade". Laurence doesn't usually get involved in gossip and tries his best to avoid office politics. But, given the evidence he has been presented with, he now believes that the manager in question is not technically competent.

But what should he do? Who should he go to? Laurence has previously had a good working relationship with this particular colleague, and was genuinely surprised at the allegations. He thinks of the potential damage it could do to the manager's reputation if it proves to be an isolated incident. He is also aware that, if he makes a complaint that is without substance, he himself could be disciplined. He doesn't know what to do. Laurence is in a dilemma.

Over to you …

13.   The Wages of Sin

Áine is a senior working on the audit of a client firm. As part of the annual audit, she has been sent to do the payroll audit. As a part of her investigations, she notices that the payroll records do not reflect all payments made. She managed to get a copy of the source labour costing documents that are used to prepare the management accounts on a monthly basis. From a quick reconciliation between payroll's records and management accounting records, she notices that the gap is not a minor one. It is potentially, in her view, material.

She makes inquiries into the matter, but cannot get to the bottom of it. Áine is concerned that there could be a major problem with significant implications, not only for the company, but for the audit firm, if it subsequently comes to light. She decides to record her findings so that they are on file, but her manager (at the review) instructs her to remove these comments from the file, despite having apprised him of her concerns. He told her not to worry about it; it wasn't a matter for her concern.

Áine still had doubts about this situation and she decides to keep the note on file. When her manager subsequently sees the note again at another follow-up meeting, he becomes agitated, ripping the note from the file. He tells Áine that he regards her behaviour as insubordinate and, if she dares to do anything like that again, she will get a written warning. Áine is in a dilemma.

Over to you ...

14.   Listen without Prejudice?

Julie, a well-regarded accountant by training, qualified 10 years ago. The reference to "by training" is deliberate, as she left practice soon after finally qualifying. She served in various positions in the construction trade, steadily and rapidly rising through the ranks to the position of procurement director for a construction company. She has been away from the coalface of day-to-day accounts for almost 10 years, though she does feel her accounting training gives her an advantage over her colleagues at times in relation to the financial statement analysis.

The company she is a director of has decided to bid for a high profile Public Private Partnership (PPP) contract to build a bridge, as well as a new portion of toll road. Though the financial nuances of PPP contracts are outside her technical ambit of expertise, the owner of the business, who is a bit of an autocrat, has told her she will be the lead financial person on the project. Finessing arguments or reasoning with him is not an easy task – he is like an iron fist inside an iron glove; he doesn't "do" nuance. He sees things quite simplistically. Julie is a qualified accountant – his company is bidding for a construction contract that needs the expertise of an accounting professional – she is that professional. All of a sudden, she is the lead consultant in putting forward a PPP bid. She knows she is completely out of her depth.

Julie is aware that to be competent in this arena she would need to have significant experience of structured finance contracts, given the complexity of computing the risk profiling these projects require. This is the problem Julie faces – though she has been working in the construction arena for several years, she has very limited experience of civil engineering, PPPs or, for that matter, the specialised financial aspects of their operation. She would go as far as to say that she has absolutely zero knowledge of PPPs, except for what she reads in the press and *Accountancy Ireland.*

Yes, she studied finance subjects for her professional exams, but that was a long time ago and, given how the world has moved on in the interim, it wouldn't be a sufficient knowledge base to brief on such a high profile project now. This issue has started to cause Julie real concern, given the sums involved. The owner of the company has also placed great expectations on Julie's advice – if the company gets this contract, they will, in his words, be "sorted" for years to come, ensuring the survival and sustainability of 150 jobs. If they don't, then who knows what will happen and, as he told Julie at the last planning meeting, "we'll know who's to blame". Julie is in a dilemma.

Over to you …

15.   Food for Thought

Laura is working on an audit of one of her firm's bigger clients, a company that manufactures ingredients and products for the bakery industry. The company makes cakes, confectionery and general bakery products. She has been working on the audit for some years. She likes this job; the clients are easy to deal with, very co-operative and the manufacturing facilities themselves are pristine. She always has to wear safety and protective clothing. It is a job that is a bit out of the ordinary, a bit of a change from the usual factories. But what makes the job more pleasurable is the straightforward and "fair dealing" approach of the clients. They are very open and transparent, eager to enhance their business at every juncture and very progressive in their outlook. As an indicator of how they do their business, they mentioned last year that they intended to implement aspects of the Global Reporting Initiative, the framework for sustainability reporting, such was their commitment as a company to sustainable development issues.

During the course of stocktake, Laura has no queries with any of the stock checked. But she has noticed something that is troubling her in relation to some mixes for product recipes. On foot of a conversation she has had with some of the production staff, a story has emerged that is somewhat at odds with the very positive messages managers have been putting out about their business. She notices a mix coming from one of the production casks that is being packed as value label for a leading supermarket. She then hangs around for five more minutes and sees the remaining mix from the same cask being packaged and finished using "fair trade" labels and stickers. Laura further notices these batches are destined for delicatessen outlets in Dublin 4. When Laura sees this, she is in a quandary.

She realises that the company is doing nothing illegal in relation to product safety. She is content that the food hygiene and safety reports for the factory are of the highest standard – all of the raw materials come from reputable sources and their provenance can be vouched for. The principal problem centres on branding and corporate responsibility concerns. As well as the fair trade issue, some of the product is sold to children and at a premium, advertised as being "ethically sourced". What's more, Laura has never seen remittances being dispatched to suppliers in the developing world.

Laura is reasonably satisfied that the company is doing nothing illegal (though she is even unsure on this matter, as the company may be in contravention of labelling regulations).

Laura has studied corporate social responsibility and corporate citizenship as part of her degree and, and asks herself whether, even if the company may be doing nothing illegal, she should do anything about it? She is satisfied that there is absolutely no health risk to consumers, so is this even anything to do with her? Or should she just leave well enough alone? From her study of CSR and corporate citizenship, she knows that, if she makes these concerns public, it could damage the company's reputation irreparably (as is often the case with food companies) and put 103 jobs at potential risk. Laura is in a dilemma.

Over to you …

16.   A Fair Day's Pay for a Fair Day's Work

Sinead had been sent out by her firm to work on a payroll audit. She never liked these types of jobs because it was very rare that any issues came to light. Given the good reputation of the client firm, it was almost like a mechanical process, always the same outcome. What's more, with financial reporting systems and software now so integrated and fine tuned, she had never discovered anything of significance. Her main concern was whether the deductions had been computed correctly. Diane, the payroll manager at the client firm, ran the system like clockwork and was conscientious to a fault. The outcome of her review of the system was the same as when she completed it previously – all payroll deductions were correct.

However, Sinead thought she would look into one of the files in greater detail. It was the file detailing payments made to temporary workers. The file appeared to have grown since the last audit was done. The client, a firm involved in manufacturing heavy plant for the construction trade, had contracted workers from an overseas firm, employing an agency in the search process. This type of arrangement appears to suit the company well. As the business owns a block of residential property the owner purchased a few years ago as an investment, it can provide accommodation for the overseas workers.

Upon reviewing the file, all of the migrant workers have, on the face of it, proper contracts; terms and conditions are appropriately and correctly stipulated. Again, Sinead is happy that the company is operating appropriately. In line with other employment contracts, there are specified numbers of hours per week. The company, however, runs a clocking-in card system. Again, all the figures stack up.

However, Sinead notices, on closer inspection, that: (i) they are working in excess of contracted hours, yet being paid at normal time, in contravention of the firm's general terms and conditions for overtime working; and (ii) there are deductions for miscellaneous services that are not clearly articulated or defined. The deductions being made for these services seem quite high as a percentage of overall deductions. She asks for explanations for these deductions from Diane, who tells her it is to do with the accommodation charges, but also stalls Sinead, saying she needs to clarify a couple of issues in relation to that. Diane tells Sinead that she will check with Brendan, the site manager, and get back to her.

Sinead busies herself with another outstanding part of the audit until she gets a response from the client. But, as a result of the initial documentation she has collected, she surmises that the following could be happening: (i) that the migrant workers are potentially being exploited by being forced to work at below their contracted rates, in addition to not being paid for overtime in a correct manner; (ii) they are being charged excessive rents for using company property to live in, possibly in contravention of their contracts; and (iii) the workers are potentially expected to work hours in excess of legal limits, a point of particular importance, given the type of equipment they are operating, which could be putting them and others at risk. Moreover, this last point could also have implications for the cover the client has in relation to public liability insurance. Should she go in, all guns blazing, or adopt a more conciliatory approach when dealing with the client? Is this even a matter for her? Sinead is in a dilemma.

Over to you …

17. "If your Name's Not on the List …"

James can remember the day he found out – it was fantastic, the culmination of years of hard work – he had passed his FAE! He was so happy to be finished his exams; it marked the end of a long process that, at times, seemed without end. The only problem was he now had to look for a job. After one tough long slog, now James was presented with another. He hoped that this one would be easier to deal with than the last one. But he wasn't going to fool himself; it was going to be tough, his friend who left last year told him there was very little out there.

He read a newspaper article that said that according to a recent survey, in recessionary times, respondents felt that it was acceptable to "enhance" CVs to make them stand out in job applications. He thought to himself, if everyone else is at it, then that's good enough for me. One of the jobs that he wanted to go for had quite specific, and exacting, short-listing criteria. The application stipulated that being a member of the Chartered Accountants Ireland was an essential requirement. "All right, I haven't applied for membership of Chartered Accountants Ireland yet, though I have passed all the exams, got the FAE and this information is absolutely valid and correct; why shouldn't I go for the job? I'm not really doing anything wrong, am I?" he tried to justify to himself. "After all, it's just a matter of timing, isn't it? It's not like I'm saying I've passed the exams when I haven't."

And so, he completed the application form and put down that he was a member of Chartered Accountants Ireland, despite the fact that he had yet to apply formally for membership. Then Barry, a friend of his from university, who had just been called to the Bar, even though he didn't have much practical experience as yet, told him what he was doing amounted to misrepresentation, or in plain English, lying. He also told him that, for a professional, lying was unforgiveable, no matter for what the purpose or intended outcome. But James was slow to take on board Barry's advice. James essentially saw getting his qualification as a process, a game to be played. Surely bending the rules once in a while was to be expected? He didn't have much time for this "ethically-based competency" stuff. His view of becoming a professional was to follow the path of least resistance. What's the right answer? What's likely to come up in the exam? Forget the "bigger picture". Focus on the next hurdle along the road. "And hurdles are only there to be manoeuvred around, aren't they?" he thought to himself.

Despite the advice of his friend Barry, James proceeded with the application. Soon a letter inviting him to interview arrives, which he reads for the time and date of the appointment. Reading the letter in more detail overleaf, his attention is drawn to the statement on it, in capital letters, that the firm will take up all references and use whatever means necessary to validate the information provided by the applicant. Moreover, applicants' attention is drawn to the fact that, even if they are appointed, if subsequent information comes to light that invalidates their application, they will be subject to immediate dismissal. This stops James in his tracks. Now that he is in the system, he is on the horns of a dilemma.

Over to you …

18. A Woman's Work?

Cathy is a newly qualified accountant working in a local accountancy practice. It would probably be classified as a micro firm, with just the partner, one secretary (Patricia), and herself. She has worked for the firm for four years. Though the pace of change has been hectic, a number of big events have happened recently. Her firm and another local small firm (though larger than her firm) have decided to merge. Although this initially was a matter of concern for the staff of both practices – some thought there would be inevitable job losses with the coming together of the firms – the partners of both assuaged any fears they had. The premises of the smaller firm would be sold off – it was mortgage-free – and the proceeds used to fund expansion plans. The logistical implications were that Cathy and her colleagues were to move to the larger office.

Initially, Cathy quite enjoyed the move. The new office was more modern, closer to the town centre and close to the gym she went to on her way to work every day. But after being there a month, she spotted what she felt to be potentially a worrying practice. Though it was an informal office atmosphere and all of the staff got on well, it appeared to Cathy that certain people had their roles and work defined by "this is the way things are done around here".

Having asked around a bit in the new office, in as unobtrusive a way as possible, about the "way things are done around here", she found out that it had long been a policy that the most junior trainees helped out with administrative duties such as posting mail, making lodgements, covering reception when required, etc. Cathy noticed that, as the accountancy practice expanded, invariably it was the female staff members who were still being asked to carry out these duties, even though there were male staff members who were equally junior. John, the male trainee, confirmed this to her when Cathy asked him, though he was oblivious to there being any issue or, for that matter, discontent. In addition, Jennifer, the daughter of one of the partners, appeared to be exempt from these duties.

Cathy is a bit taken aback at what she sees happening around her, but is confused as to what she ought to do about it. What could she do to change things? For that matter, do people want things to change and should she even try? Cathy is in a dilemma.

Over to you …

PART III

Further Cases in Business and Ethics

by Hugh McBride
Senior Lecturer in Business Studies
Galway–Mayo Institute of Technology

(Suggested solutions to these cases are available from your lecturer.)

Kilaney Ltd

Mary Lenihan has been working in the family business, Kilaney Ltd, for the last 10 months. She is 29 years old and a social science graduate. Following her studies, she worked for two years with a charity organisation in Africa. She then spent two years in Australia working in part-time jobs and travelling. Following this, she moved to London, got married, had two children and worked as an administrator in a support agency for minorities. Eighteen months ago, her grandmother died, leaving Mary a 22% share-ownership in Kilaney Ltd. With the encouragement of her parents and her husband she decided to move home and take up an executive director role in the business.

Kilaney was established by Mary's grandfather over 40 years ago. It manufactures chemical compounds and in recent years has specialised in supplying the cosmetics sector with compounds for skin-cream products. It has a mixed base of customers ranging from multinationals to SMEs. Most of its business is through fixed-term contractual orders. The company is located in Mayo and is the main employer in the local area. Its significance to the local economy has been emphatically emphasised by a number of factory closures in the region over the last two years. The local rate of unemployment is currently estimated at 12%.

Kilaney has been managed for six years by Mary's two older brothers, Joe and Peter. They both went straight into the business from school and had taken over executive control after the retirement of their father. They each own 20% of the company's shares. Of the remaining shares, 23% are owned by their parents and 15% by a bank. The bank had agreed to convert a loan into shares four years previously following trading difficulties which necessitated a financial restructuring. At that time, a recovery strategy was implemented and this has worked reasonably well. Each of the shareholders has a seat on the Board, which also includes two non-shareholding, non-executive directors. One of these is a prominent local merchant and the other is a retired professor of chemistry who was appointed on the recommendation of a State industry-support agency. The Board is chaired by Mary's father.

Mary's homecoming has not worked out as she expected. Shortly after the move, her husband was injured in a car accident and is unlikely to return to work in the near future. In the context of her role in the company, Mary quickly realised how little she knew about the business and has faced a steep learning curve. In addition, her relationship with her brothers has steadily worsened. It seems that they resent the fact of her inheritance and her attempt to engage actively in management of the company. Joe's facetious remark, made shortly after her return, to "trust us and leave it to the professionals to do the real work" was, in retrospect, ominous.

The issue now under discussion by the Board threatens to cause a major family rift. Mary has expressed concern about the renewal of a contract to supply a customer, Nimh Ltd, with a particular compound for a further period of two years. The difficulty for Mary is that this compound is used by Nimh as a key component in the manufacture of skin-cream products for sale in Africa. These products are used mainly by women as bleaching agents to lighten the colour of their skin and hair, for the treatment of skin ailments and as an antiseptic. Mary wants Kilaney to turn down the contract and her brothers have reacted furiously to the suggestion. Mary's parents have indicated a level of sympathy with her point of view.

Mary explained that there is incontrovertible evidence that the skin-cream products are toxic and that the risks associated with their constant use are significant. They have been described by one health research organisation as a "serious health hazard" possibly causing skin disease, kidney failure, foetal damage and cancer. Following extensive lobbying by development NGOs, a ban on the sale and import of these products within the EU is imminent. At present, some of these products are openly available for sale in ethnic shops around Ireland. Mary argued that the products represent a form of what she calls "commercial racism". The demand for the products, she explained, arose from an exploitation and manipulation of the deep-seated insecurities of poor black women who were made to feel inadequate in a world which portrayed lighter-skinned women with straight blond hair as the role model for female success. "I don't want us to have any part in this type of dirty exploitative business", she declared. "It's indefensible for us to profit from generating misery; for us to be part of the manufacture of products for export to Africa which are deemed unfit for sale here."

In response, Peter was incandescent with rage:

> "You might not like it, but it is this type of business that has kept this company afloat the last four years. This contract may be essential for our survival; if we don't take it, we will certainly have to lay off about 30% of the workforce immediately. Will you explain to the workers that your moral scruples are costing them their jobs? Some of them are young and have big mortgages. There isn't anything else for them around here. Some of the older ones might never find work again. Let's get a few facts straight here. First, we are contracting to sell a chemical compound, not a dangerous skin cream. The logic of your argument is that no one should supply inputs to the tobacco or the armaments or the nuclear industries. What our customers do with the compound is not our responsibility. Secondly, we are doing nothing illegal and neither, incidentally, is Nimh. The ban you refer to

relates only to the sale of these creams; it will still be perfectly legal to make these products within the EU for export. And the countries to which these products are exported have not banned them. Thirdly, if we don't take up this contract, our competitors will. We will lose out and it won't change anything. Finally, the State agencies seem to find nothing wrong with this type of business. Both Nimh and ourselves have received generous grants of Irish taxpayers' money and various other supports. Indeed, the Trade Minister on her recent visit here praised us for continuing to provide jobs in an area where they are desperately needed."

Then Joe spoke:

"Listen Mary, while you were swanning around college and then around the world, Peter and I were here working long hours doing whatever was needed to sustain the business. For the last four years it has been about survival. Our dog-eat-dog industry requires a cut-throat attitude. I really resent an Anita Roddick wannabee, and one with no business experience to boot, trying to tell us how to run our affairs. Business is business and you do what is necessary; if you can't stand the dirt, then don't play in the muck. Business is dirty work sometimes, but you have to be prepared for that if you want to succeed. The campaign against Nimh's products has been funded by manufacturers of so-called 'natural' cosmetics. They are hardly an independent voice and the research you mention is far from conclusive and its objectivity is questionable. I expect that soon their campaign will be extended to criticising all chemical-based cosmetic products. And don't you think that you are being somewhat patronising towards African women? That you are exhibiting a form of subtle racism? It may interest you to know that Nimh is fully-owned by three African women. As I understand it, the demand for their products arises because many of Nimh's customers can't afford the more expensive Western brands; so it's these cheap ones or nothing. There is no alternative for the poor in Africa. And in this regard, I notice you have nothing to say about their use as an effective and cheap treatment for skin ailments and as an antiseptic. And just to follow up on one of Peter's points, the banks and the government have obviously no problem with this type of trade. They have been willing to finance both Nimh and us. Why should we be expected to apply so-called higher moral standards than the financial institutions, than the government and than anyone else in the industry?"

Mary was taken aback by the vehemence of her brothers' remarks, but responded:

"Don't try to bully me. This is a Board meeting and I remind you that I am the largest single shareholder and will be treated with respect. We must recognise an obligation to those affected by our products. Selfish economic gain should not be our only guide or the only criteria we apply in our decision-making. How we behave in trying to make profits is important. We have a basic duty to protect and promote the well-being of others. If we put our heads together, I'm sure we can identify alternative and viable product markets for the company. And one further point: it will hardly seem like good business when this gets into the national media. Bad publicity resulting in a bad image and reputation will hardly help us in our dealings with the multinationals or in winning new business in future. A piece about Nimh's products has already been mentioned in at least one of the national newspapers and the story is likely to grow in significance after the EU ban is implemented."

At this point, the prominent local merchant spoke in an avuncular tone:

"Duty is an admirable screen to creep behind when we wish to avoid doing what ought to be done. Indeed, what must be done? Survival is the issue here, not gain. There will be plenty of time to worry about moral niceties when the company is strong again. Meantime, we must continue with this contract."

The representative of the bank and the professor both nodded sagely.

Required

Discuss the issues arising in the above case. What would you advise? Explain your reasons.

Shane Nolan

Shane Nolan is in the third month of his appointment as East Africa logistics manager for the UK multinational corporation BR plc. He is based in the port city of Monberri and his responsibilities include the purchase, import and storage of the raw materials, spare parts and equipment required by BR's manufacturing plants in the region. BR is one of the biggest importers through Monberri port. The logistics operation is crucial to the success of the manufacturing plants.

Shane has just encountered his first serious problem since taking up the post. Normally, it takes four to seven days to process a container through the port, from landing to release. However, the processing of a number of BR containers with vital spare parts has been delayed by the Port Authority. Mr Phiri, the port manager, has indicated that the "problems" could take up to eight weeks to resolve and in the meantime he cannot guarantee the safety of the consignment. Monberri has a deserved reputation for theft from through trade and for corrupt practices by port officials. Phiri has told Shane that "ways and means" might be found to speed up the release of the containers but that this would require some "generous goodwill gesture" by Shane as "a facilitating mechanism".

Shane discussed the situation with Fr Peter, a Jesuit priest who has lived in Monberri for 17 years.

"He is asking for a bribe. Unfortunately, that is the usual way business is done in the country at present. You pay Phiri and all the port officials down the line get a cut. Of course, bribery is officially denounced and it does greatly undermine the potential for long term development. But, as they say, in the long-term we are all dead. The officials at the port are paid lousy wages and bribery is the only avenue open to them to survive. You would probably do the same in their position."

Prior to leaving London, Shane attended a one-day ethics seminar for BR overseas executives. The CEO had chaired the afternoon session. BR has a written Code of Ethics to which management at all levels are required to commit themselves. It specifically prohibits the payment of bribes. However, during a discussion at the seminar, Shane was left with the impression that senior management were equivocal in their attitude. Rather than a clear message of "don't do it", the signal seemed to be that bribery may be unavoidable in some countries but "don't get caught doing it". In fact, senior management's primary concern seemed to be avoiding adverse publicity in the UK media.

Shane had joined BR after graduating from college and intended making a long-term career with the company. He is considered to be a rising managerial star. His appointment in Monberri is for three years and he can then look forward to a plum promotion. Shane and his wife Ann had settled quickly into the rhythm of life in Monberri. As well as a generous salary and overseas allowance, he was provided with a brand new Landcruiser and a substantial, colonial-style house. BR paid for the domestic staff at the house, including a cook and a gardener. Shane and Ann were also given fully-paid membership of the very exclusive Monberri Lawn Tennis & Polo Club.

Mitch Blackmore is BR's longest-serving manager in the region and headed up one of the manufacturing facilities. He has advised Shane to pay the bribe:

> "That is what everyone else does. That is what London really expects you to do, although they won't say so. It's a normal cost of the business game in these parts. All the guys in power at the port, including Phiri, are members of the ruling ZAFF political party. You pay the bribe by writing a cheque payable to ZAFF. The internal auditors in London rarely pick up on these things and even if they do it can be passed off as a legitimate political donation. BR's ethics code doesn't apply out here and everyone understands that. Rumour has it on the corporate grapevine that it might not even apply much in the UK!"

Mitch thought Shane's suggestion of seeking advice from London was naive:

> "They don't want to be bothered with this. They expect you to do the job out here. Look, if those spare parts aren't out of the port in three weeks, operations are going to shut down. The facilities managers are going to be mightily angry if that happens. Apart from the potential impact on our bonuses, we will have to lay off hundreds of workers. Think of the hardship that will cause for them and their families. If you get all 'goody-goody', it could hurt a lot of people. Sure, you could force the issue and refuse to pay the bribe. That may change things for a while and go down well officially and in the media. But it won't do your career prospects any good and it won't solve the problem of corruption."

Shane remained uncertain about what to do. He felt uneasy about compromising himself by paying the bribe. He remembered that BR had threatened to move the logistics operation to South Africa in 1996 in an effort to force a clampdown on corruption at Monberri. That had generated a lot of positive publicity for BR at the time. However, Mitch was dismissive of that episode:

> "The company could move operations south any time, no problem. But it's cheaper for them to operate out of Monberri even with the bribes and the theft. What happened in '96 was the kind of public display of corporate moral outrage that happens from time to time. The external auditors were unhappy with the scale of the so-called political donations and began asking questions. The guys in London feigned shock at the discovery. A few managers were scapegoated and hung out to dry. The port authorities cleaned up their act for a while under pressure from the publicity and BR's threat to move. But slowly, over time, normal corrupt practices resumed."

Required

Discuss the issues arising in the above case. What would you advise Shane to do? Explain your reasons.

Rachel Forde

Rachel Forde qualified as a Chartered Accountant just over one year ago. Following this, she joined a prestigious international firm of management consultants. Rachel is ambitious, self-confident, energetic and a technically gifted accountant. As evidence of her ability, she was actively recruited by the consultancy firm and her current salary is amongst the highest of her peers. Her professional goal is to become the chief financial officer and executive director of a publicly quoted company within 15 years. In this regard, she considers that the work experience she will get with the consultancy firm should prove invaluable. Furthermore, her CV will be greatly enhanced as a result of working for such a high-profile and internationally prestigious firm.

Her current assignment involves a three-month placement with Flog Ltd, a large unquoted company. The company is just over seven years old and has grown rapidly since its incorporation. At its current rate of development, it expects to be in a position to consider a stock market flotation within two years. The founder of the business remains the major shareholder and the chief executive. Rachel's assignment involves an evaluation of the financial planning and control systems leading to recommendations for improvement.

In her fifth week on the job, Rachel discovered a series of invoices from a building company for work supposedly carried out on behalf of Flog. The amounts seemed excessive and further investigation revealed that much of the work was in fact related to the personal properties of the senior management team and of one significant supplier. It seemed clear to Rachel that the invoices had been falsified.

She approached the chief executive about the matter and he was not at all surprised.

> "I instructed the building company to invoice us in this way. They had no problem with this. We are worth a lot of business to them so they are willing to play ball."

When Rachel pointed out to him that the practice was unethical and illegal, he laughed and told her to "stuff her ethics. I have a business to run." He advised her not to worry about the matter and to continue with the good work she had carried out to date. "The auditors had no problem with it, so why should you?" he asked rhetorically.

Rachel informed her immediate boss at the consultancy firm about what transpired. He also advised her to let the matter lie. He reminded her that Flog was a valuable client and that the chief executive of Flog was a personal friend of a number of the senior partners in the consultancy. He explained to Rachel that her work to date was considered excellent and that the feedback from clients had all been positive. However, Rachel got the distinct feeling that he was hinting strongly that her prospects at the consultancy firm could be greatly damaged if she pursued the matter further. He added:

> "No one likes to stir up trouble in this game. It's damaging to business, to reputations and to careers. Flog has really done nothing unusual. Such minor amendments to invoices is a common enough business practice. It's up to the auditors to police that. Essentially, it's nothing to do with us; it's not what we are paid for. Consultancy is a business like any other. Success is about satisfied customers. This may involve cutting a few corners, turning a blind eye now and again, but everyone in the game accepts this as a matter of course. Everyone does it. My advice to you is to forget this whole thing."

Required

Explain the ethical issues arising in the above situation and advise Rachel as to the course of action she should take.

Hugh McMahon

Hugh McMahon, the financial controller of Walker Ltd, has worked at the company for 18 months. He has recently been authorised by the Board to purchase, install, test and implement new computer hardware and software to drive the company's information systems. The supplier chosen would also be contractually bound to provide an after-sale service for a four-year period, this to be reviewed at that time. Hugh has received two formal bids for the project, both of which appear to meet the specified functionality requirements. One of the bids, however, would involve a much higher initial outlay for Walker. The higher bid was received from a local company, MR Ltd and the owner, Joe Coy, was one of Hugh's long-time friends. Hugh had phoned Joe explaining the situation and had suggested he lower his bid if he wanted to win the contract. The following conversation then took place:

Joe: Listen Hugh, it is really important to us that we win the contract, but at the price we have already bid. It may be the key to us obtaining venture capital finance, which is critical for our continued development. At the moment, the negotiations with the potential investors are at a delicate stage. Your contract could tip the balance. And if we don't get the finance, I see difficult times ahead for us.

Hugh: Surely it would be worse if you didn't win our contract at all? And I find it hard to believe that one contract, even one as relatively large as ours, could be of such critical importance.

Joe: True. But, as you know, I was hoping to cash in some of my shares and step back from the day-to-day operations of the business very soon. The venture capital investment is vital in that regard. And just as an aside, with the venture capital in place, I would finally be able to bring you on that golfing holiday to Portugal that I promised would happen if ever I struck it rich.

Hugh: I suppose the fact that you are a local company may prove to be an advantage. You would certainly be in a better position to fulfil the on-going after-sale service obligations: if anything went wrong, you would at least be easy to get hold of, unlike the other company bidding for the contract who are from Budapest. That difference might be a justification for the higher bid.

Joe: From Budapest? All the more reason to award us the contract. Surely we should all be trying to support local industry and keep jobs at home, especially given the current economic situation?

Hugh: That is a point. It can't be wrong to support your own. And I doubt if the foreign company will make a fuss if they don't win the bid. Indeed, it is unlikely that anyone will raise any questions at all. And if anyone does, sure I can justify accepting your bid on the basis of the potential better after-sale service. I think you should expect to be booking that golfing holiday for later this year.

Required

Do you agree with Hugh's decision to award the contract to MR Ltd.? Explain your reasons with specific reference to expected standards of ethical conduct.

Target Ltd

John is the financial controller of Target Ltd. The company is based in a midlands town and is one of the major employers in the area. In addition to providing full-time employment for 83 people, Target also provides significant part-time employment on a seasonal basis. This fits in well with the slack period in farming which remains a key element of the economic and social fabric of the region.

The company is 12 years old and was originally started by a brother and sister, Pete and Marie. They came from a family of well-known business people in the town and other members of the family invested in the fledgling company. The company remains mainly family-owned. The Board is made up entirely of family members, as is most of the senior management team. John joined Target shortly after the start-up and he owns a small number of shares in the company. He is 44-years-old and has two daughters, aged 8 and 6. In the early days of the company, John was very friendly with Pete and they socialised a lot together. But since the birth of his children, John rarely goes out socially. Pete remains a bachelor and is still very much a "man about the town".

The company designs and manufactures computer-based video games and machines that are installed mainly in arcades, pubs and cafés throughout the country. The sector is lightly regulated and competition from overseas has become fierce in recent times. Target's market share and profit margins have been in steady decline for the last two years. Games typically have a life cycle of 18–24 months. One of the key success factors in the industry is providing innovative, unique, visually stimulating and fast-paced games using super-real imagery, high-definition colour graphics and participant interaction.

Just over a year previously, the Board recognised the need to adopt a new strategic approach to the market in order to halt the decline and ensure long-term survival. Towards this end, they recruited Mark as an adviser to senior management. His main responsibility is to undertake in-depth strategic analysis, identify directions for the future and support the development of new ideas. Mark is Pete's cousin and has worked as a senior marketing executive at a number of multinational technology companies in the United States.

Mark's first set of recommendations were for specific changes to existing games based on market research he had carried out. He identified the primary market as being 11–15-year-old males. His initial research showed that "this demographic" wanted more violent action, richer graphics, multiple levels of difficulty and more realistic sound effects. The research showed that certain sounds and tones stimulated a more active response than others. Target's designers were able to quickly incorporate most of these features into the games and there was an immediate and noticeable positive impact on sales and profits as a result.

In continuing research, Mark had found that the consumer's level of intensity increased as the game's intensity level increased. He suggested an amendment where, at a particular point in the game, the consumer is asked to put in multiple coins. A player who wanted to move to a higher level of difficulty would have to insert two additional coins; to play the final level, three additional coins would be needed. This idea was also introduced and again, sales improved. John, like other members of the senior management team, was pleased by the improvement in market performance. However, he was surprised by a passage in Mark's research report suggesting that the customers became quickly hypnotized by the game and it was in this context that they were willing to put in additional coins when instructed to do so. Many customers exhibited the same symptoms as compulsive gamblers and the report recommended that Target exploit the opportunity this provided.

Mark's latest report has suggested making further changes to the games, varying the nature and intensity of the fast-action violence, relating it more specifically to "real life" and introducing a sexual element. The games would focus on scenarios in which the goal was to destroy an enemy before being destroyed. One variation was to be modelled on the situation in Iraq, another on an urban inter-gang and inter-ethnic fight scenario. In each case, the player would simulate direct involvement in the fighting and in activities such as high-speed chases in stolen cars. The latest virtual reality technology would be applied to give players the sensation of being "really in the game". Recognising that most of the customers were male, Mark has proposed incorporating various female characters. One variation would involve a character selectively removing items of her clothing and taunting the player, depending on performance. A win at the highest level of the game left her nude and destroyed. Finally, Mark has also suggested introducing games specifically designed for girls in the same age group. This was a "neglected market which is not at all catered for". The games would be based on the same types of scenarios but the main protagonists would now be female. "To show we are not in the least bit sexist", the report stated, "the ladies will have an opportunity to humiliate and destroy some male characters." The test market results showed that these proposed changes promised dramatic success.

At a meeting of senior management, John expressed concerns about the latest proposals and about the earlier changes introduced. "These new games are a long way from our traditional products. I know they have enabled us to recover our position in the market and I have no doubt that the latest proposals will also be successful in this regard. But I have misgivings about exploiting gambling, violence, prejudice and sex. I wouldn't want my daughters or their boyfriends playing these games and I'm not sure I would even want them to know I was involved in promoting them."

Mark responded that Target was only satisfying a defined need in a lucrative market. This was the direction the industry and society was taking, whether John liked it or not. "Morality," he said, "represents the way we would like the world to work, but business should only concern itself with the way the world actually is." Pete then intervened to remind the meeting about the precarious position of the business. He mentioned the on-going decline in farming and how the town would need to have work available to take up the slack. The on-going improvements to the games would help secure Target's long-term survival and provide an opportunity to expand and compete internationally. He expressed surprise at John's doubts and suggested that perhaps he was letting his "personal, middle-aged prejudice and innate conservatism interfere with his commercial judgement and his responsibility towards the well-being of the company. You should get out more and see what our customers are really up to."

Required

Discuss the ethical issues arising in the above case. What would you advise John to do? Explain your reasons.

The Dean's Dilemma

The Dean had called the meeting to try and resolve the issue of what mark to award a student for an undergraduate dissertation. The college operated the following system for marking.

The dissertation supervisor and a second reader both marked the work. The supervisor was known to the second reader (not least because of the student practice of thanking them in the document) but the second reader was supposed to be anonymous. The marks were submitted separately and it was the job of the dissertation coordinator to follow up on any differences. Generally, the marks tended to be broadly similar and the coordinator had little difficulty in getting the agreement of the markers to "split the difference". In some cases involving marginal award levels, a discussion between the markers was usually sufficient to resolve the issue. From time to time, however, a more serious issue arose such as in the current case. This generally happened when both markers awarded hugely different grades. In the current case, the supervisor, Marie, had given the student 75% (a first class honour) and the second marker, Sean, had awarded 50% (a pass). The procedure in these cases was that the coordinator informed both markers about the situation and then a third anonymous reader was appointed. This usually provided a basis for negotiating an acceptable compromise.

Marie was a highly-respected senior lecturer and was a "hot-tip" for the Dean's job that was to be shortly interviewed for, following the retirement of the current Dean. She was widely published in all the best international journals, had served with distinction on both the Academic Council and the Governing Body and was part of a number of college-wide strategic task forces set up by the president. Sean had worked at the college as a full-time lecturer for four years and was hoping to complete his doctorate within a year.

The third reader appointed was Pete, a lecturer in his first year at the college and on a short-term contract. Sean got to know this because Pete told him. They had been friendly for a long time having been in the same class at college. Pete approached him one day and told him that he had read the dissertation and had initially felt it to be of a pass standard. However, following discussions with Marie, he had realised that it probably merited at least a 2:1 honours mark. Sean and he had been friendly for a long time and he didn't want any bad feeling between them, which was why, he explained, he was telling Sean what happened. He hoped that this would resolve the matter without any "unpleasantness".

Sean was a little disturbed by the conversation with Pete, especially the fact that Marie had talked to him prior to his submission of a mark. He wondered if Pete felt in some way threatened by Marie, particularly as he hoped to apply for one of the permanent positions that were shortly due to be advertised. Marie enjoyed a reputation for being "persuasive" and for getting her own way. Sean respected her as an academic, but in their limited contact he had never warmed to her on a personal level. He felt she was a self-serving and calculating person, powerfully driven by a curious combination of insecurity and overbearing ambition.

Shortly after his meeting with Pete, the coordinator approached Sean with a proposal to resolve the difference. Marie was agreeable to award the student 69% for the dissertation. The coordinator explained that this represented a major climb-down for Marie and left her in an embarrassing situation with the student. She had taken a keen and active interest in the student's progress – more than might normally be expected – and had apparently intimated to the student that the dissertation was of a 1:1 standard. Sean refused to amend his mark. He also asked the coordinator how he had come to appoint such an inexperienced member of staff as Pete to be the third reader; and he wanted to know how it was that Marie knew the identity of the third reader before Pete had even submitted a mark, and, how Pete had known that he, Sean, was the second reader. The coordinator responded evasively by asking Sean why he was so down on this particular student. "What difference will it make anyway?" he asked.

It was as a result of the impasse that the Dean had called a meeting of all parties involved to resolve the issue. Sean was first asked to explain his refusal to amend his mark in any way. He explained that the dissertation topic was in a specific area in which he had considerable expertise. He pointed out that, despite her considerable talents, it was a topic somewhat outside Marie's disciplinary area and that this perhaps explained the difference in evaluation. He went on to explain that there was a considerable body of well-established literature that was not even referred to in the dissertation and that the tone of the work was one of "amateurish speculations and imaginings". Sean admitted it was a well-presented piece of work but it "flattered to deceive" and contained little of substance. Indeed, it was not even clear that the student fully understood the topic and its implications. "It seemed at times as if the student felt she had discovered something new which is really something long established." It was worth a pass grade, he concluded and nothing more.

Marie began with a sarcastic remark noting that "her young colleague was questioning her academic competence and her ability to supervise and grade student dissertations". She disagreed with Sean's analysis and pointed out that two out of the three readers felt the award should be at least a 2:1. She pointedly asked Pete to confirm this view to which he muttered assent. She explained that the student in question was a person of great ability and commitment and that it had been a pleasure to supervise her work. She referred to her long experience and that she "knew a 1:1 when I see it". She explained that she had taken Sean's views on board and was willing to compromise and award a 2:1, but that Sean had shown no such flexibility and reciprocal respect for her judgement. Finally, she explained that there were circumstances that Sean did not know about which may be of significance. "The student had some serious medical issues during the year but she struggled bravely through them. She also intends to go on to continue her studies at Brown College in the States. She has been accepted but this is conditional on her obtaining an overall 2:1 award, including in her dissertation. So there is a lot riding on our judgement."

Sean felt that Marie was making herself the issue and that the circumstances referred to should be considered extraneous to their current deliberations. He made no comment on this, however.

The Dean then spoke. He confirmed what Marie said about the student's circumstances, "knowing the family as I do". He explained how keen he was that the issue be resolved before the Examination Board.

> "We all remember last year's events and the chaos at the meetings. I want no more such washing of our dirty linen in public and no more inter-personal rows surfacing at that forum. Problems must be resolved beforehand and, if necessary, individuals

will have to bite the bullet and keep their own counsel at the meetings. People have to put aside their own agendas in the interests of the college and the greater good. We are on show at those meetings and I want them to run smoothly. What I propose in this case is as follows. As there are two votes in favour of awarding a 2:1 that is what we will do. We will give the student 69%, but we will send the dissertation to one of the external examiners for moderation. That seems fair to all parties. Now, there has been enough time and discussion on this matter already so I propose we leave it at that until we hear from the extern."

At that he declared the meeting ended.

Sean was very unhappy. He knew that the extern to whom the dissertation would most likely be sent was a friend of Marie. Furthermore, in the two years since his appointment, he had not queried any of the marks awarded in the dissertations or indeed at all. He was generally sympathetic to suggestions made by the internal examiners at the Board meetings regarding amendments to marks.

Sean was also concerned that the 69% would be brought up at the Board meeting to a 70% as generally tended to be the case. He often wondered whether examiners deliberately avoided responsibility by the award of such threshold marks leaving it to the Board to make the hard choice.

Required

Discuss any ethical issues raised in the case.

Mind your Language
(With apologies to Philip Roth)

At the start of the second semester, Pat started teaching a new group of students with whom he had no previous contact. There were two students on the list who did not appear for the first two weeks. Pat asked the class whether anyone knew where they were and was told that "they had gone away". To which he remarked good-humouredly: "Ah, intrepid travellers are they? How nice for them to take to the road, anois teacht an Earraigh".

The following week Pat was summoned by the head of school. An official complaint had been lodged by a student claiming that Pat had spoken derogatorily about her in class. She was from a Traveller background and was finding it hard enough to get through college without the added barrier of racism. The student had been to see the counsellor who was willing, with the student's agreement, to attest to her difficulties. She was also supported by a number of lecturers who were active in a Traveller support group outside the college and who were involved in a self-styled "concerned lecturers" campaigning group within the college. As one of their projects, they had initiated a "stamp-out-racism" campaign on campus which had since been subsumed under the partnership process.

"Listen Pat," said the Head, "I know that you are in no way racist in attitude. This was probably an innocent mistake. But in the current PC climate we must all exercise particular care. The student has agreed to withdraw her complaint if you apologise publicly to her in front of the class and also write a letter to her to that effect. That would end the affair quickly and no one loses out."

Before answering the Head, Pat enquired about the student's academic track record. "Not that it is of any direct relevance," said the Head, "but she has just about scraped through to date with a certain amount of sympathy and leeway from Exam Boards. Her attendance has not been great but it seems that lecturers have been willing to give her the benefit of the doubt given her background." Pat thought for a moment then responded as follows:

> "I am not going to make any apology because I have done nothing wrong. I knew nothing of this student until today. I intended no comment on her background, nor could I have. It was a mildly humorous remark, a part of ordinary everyday discourse. Is the word 'traveller' in its traditional usage now to be outlawed; annexed by a lobby group in the service of their specific purposes? I refuse to be bullied into compromising my dignity and my academic position because of a bogus threat. I think this student's academic track record may be very relevant here. It seems to me that this is an attempt to cow me into helping her scrape through later in the year."

The Head listened with mounting concern.

> "Standing on your dignity solves nothing Pat. What difference will it make if you make the apology? This will then be forgotten about next week. But if you don't, be aware that there will be powerful forces mobilised against you, not least the concerned lecturers group who seem to have adopted this girl's case. Are you prepared for all the hassle that will come your way? And for the possibility that the case might go against you and all the consequences that entails? At the very least, this won't look good on your record and could tell against you if, for example, you were to apply for a promotion post. This could cause bad feeling in the school and we don't need that just now. Think what the newspapers could do with the story if it leaked out. Why don't you just make the damn apology and have done with it?"

Required

Discuss any ethical issues raised in the case.